P9-CBI-540

HAITI EARTHQUAKE
SURVIVAL STORIES

BY MARNE VENTURA

Published by The Child's World®
1980 Lookout Drive • Mankato, MN 56003-1705
800-599-READ • www.childsworld.com

Acknowledgments
The Child's World®: Mary Berendes, Publishing Director
Red Line Editorial: Design, editorial direction, and production
Photographs ©: Ramon Espinosa/AP Images, cover, 1, 12; iStockphoto, 6; Shutterstock
Images, 9, 20, 26; Dieu Nalio Chery/AP Images, 10; Roberto Schmidt/AFP Photo/
Getty Images, 15; Michael Francis McElroy/ZumaPress/Newscom, 16; Esteban Felix/
AP Images, 18; Christophe Calais/Corbis, 23; United States Agency for International
Development, 24; Alison Wright/Corbis, 25; Matthew McDermott/AmeriCares/Polaris/
Newscom, 29

ISBN 9781634074230

LCCN 2015946311

Printed in the United States of America
Mankato, MN
December, 2015
PA02288

ABOUT THE AUTHOR
Marne Ventura is the author of 24 books for kids. She loves writing about
nature, science, technology, health, and crafts. She is a former elementary
school teacher, and she holds a master's degree in education. Marne lives
with her husband on the central coast of California, where she survived the
San Simeon earthquake in 2003.

TABLE OF
CONTENTS

DISASTER STRIKES

January 12, 2010, began like a normal day in Port-au-Prince, Haiti. The weather was warm and clear. Men, women, and children bustled about the city as usual. The crowded capital sits on the west side of an island between the Caribbean Sea and the Atlantic Ocean. Most people in the city live in **poverty**. Many are crowded into badly built concrete houses. About one-half of the homes have no bathrooms. Only one-third have tap water.

Just before 5:00 p.m., the ground began to shake. Experts estimate the movement lasted 35 to 60 seconds. Buildings toppled to the ground, crushing and trapping people. Thousands of Haitians ran into the streets, many crying and screaming. The sky was gray with dust.

Experts knew a large **fault** ran through Port-au-Prince. But the last major earthquake to hit the area had occurred more than 200 years earlier. Most scientists were surprised when the strong quake struck in 2010. Its **epicenter** was 10 miles (16 km) to the southwest of the capital. Forty **aftershocks** shook Haiti during the next 24 hours. The shaking continued to destroy unstable homes and shops. Schools fell down. There was not enough medical help for the amount of hurt people. Phones stopped working. Relatives did not know whether their loved ones were safe.

The earthquake caused hundreds of thousands of deaths and injuries. Yet out of the **rubble**, people had inspiring stories of survival.

FAST FACTS

Time
- 4:53 p.m. on January 12, 2010

Size
- Magnitude 7.0

Total Deaths
- Estimated from 220,000 to 316,000

People Displaced
- More than one million

Effect on Schools
- More than one-fourth damaged or destroyed

Financial Response
- $13 billion was raised

Chapter 1

PAYING IT FORWARD

Twenty-one-year-old Junior Bernard was born and raised in the small Haitian town of Jérémie. He grew up poor and was often hungry. He decided at a young age that he wanted to go to the United States to get an education.

Bernard began to memorize words from an English dictionary. When American workers visited his town, he practiced speaking to them. Soon, he knew enough English to work as an **interpreter** for visitors from the United States. That is how he met Bill Barr, a volunteer from New Jersey. Barr was in Jérémie working for an organization that brings medical help to Haitians in need. Barr understood Bernard's dream. He could see that Bernard was working hard to make it come true. Barr said he would help Bernard come to the United States.

On January 12, 2010, Bernard was asleep when the earthquake hit. He woke with a start. "It felt like the whole earth, like

◀ **Many homes in Port-au-Prince were poorly made and close together, making the damage of the quake even worse.**

the whole city, was going to fall in a big hole," he said later. "Everyone was crying. People were yelling."[1] Bernard was staying with relatives in Port-au-Prince when the earthquake struck. He was there to get the paperwork he needed to go to school in the United States.

When the ground finally stopped shaking, Bernard walked outside. He did not recognize the neighborhood. No houses were left standing. Bodies were lying in the streets. He had to help.

Bernard contacted Barr after the earthquake. Barr sent money so Bernard could help earthquake victims. Bernard bought medicine, clothes, and food with the money. He brought his goods to a nearby port, where people were exiting two big boats. Bernard distributed his items to people affected by the earthquake as they got off the boats. He did the same at a bus stop.

Bernard also borrowed a camera to take pictures of the **devastation**. He sent them to Barr and other Americans to show the conditions in Haiti.

A friend in the United States showed Bernard's message to the dean of students at Alvernia University in Pennsylvania. The dean was impressed with Bernard and wanted to help him make a better life for himself and for others. He told Bernard that the university would pay for him to attend school in the United States.

Bernard became a business major at Alvernia University. Now he works as a speaker. He tells people the story of his life. He wants them to know that if he could rise from a poor, hungry boy in Haiti to a college graduate, they can, too. He hopes to help people the way Barr and the university helped him.

SHIFTING SURFACE

Two plates in Earth's crust moved, or slipped, in opposite directions to cause the earthquake in Haiti. This type of plate boundary is known as a strike-slip fault.

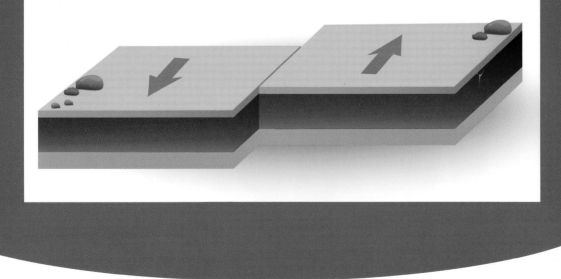

Chapter 2

RESCUED AT LAST

Darlene Etienne was at her cousin's home in Port-au-Prince when the ground began to shake. Darlene was staying with her cousin to attend a nearby high school. When the quake struck, the home fell down around Darlene. Dust from the crumbling cement filled the air and covered her. When the shaking stopped, she found herself trapped. She had just enough space around her to lie down. But she could not dig her way out of the **debris**.

Darlene called for help. No one answered. Where were her cousin and his wife? Were rescue workers coming? Darlene waited and waited. With nothing to eat or drink, she grew weaker and weaker. Occasionally, she heard voices nearby. Filled with hope that people had come to save her, she called with all her might. But the voices moved away. Nobody heard her cries for help.

Darlene waited for two long weeks. She never gave up. On the fifteenth day, she was so weak from thirst and hunger that

◀ **Darlene (center) moved to Port-au-Prince just nine days before the earthquake.**

2010 EARTHQUAKE TIMELINE

- January 12: Quake strikes at 4:53 p.m.

- January 13: Haitian prime minister reports more than 100,000 deaths.

- January 14: Other countries send rescue and medical teams to help.

- January 15: Many people are without food and shelter in Port-au-Prince.

- January 16: Death estimates are raised to 200,000.

- January 17: Thousands of people are reported homeless.

- January 18: Many people flee from Port-au-Prince in search of food and water.

- January 19: The United Nations sends troops to stop violence and looting.

- January 20: More than 120 people have been rescued from the rubble.

- January 27: Darlene Etienne is found and rescued.

she could barely make a sound. She did her best to call out. To her surprise, this time, she got an answer. A neighbor who was walking near the rubble heard her and called back. Darlene told him her name. She gave him the phone number of her family in

◄ Rescue workers carry Darlene away from the rubble 15 days after the earthquake.

13

her hometown. He promised to contact her family and call for rescue workers.

Soon, Darlene could hear many voices above her. She heard the sounds of workers pulling away the broken concrete and pieces of the building that were trapping her. Within 45 minutes, she could see daylight. But she was so weak from hunger and thirst that she needed help getting up. "Thank you," she whispered, as the rescuers lifted her from the ruins.[2] Hundreds of onlookers cheered. The crew gave her oxygen, water to drink, and candy. They wrapped her in foil blankets and strapped her onto a stretcher. Darlene cried tears of happiness.

The rescue team took Darlene to a hospital onboard a ship. Doctors know that most people do not survive without water for more than ten days. They were amazed that Darlene held out for more than two weeks. Her left leg was broken, and she was badly **dehydrated**. But she was going to make a full recovery. Darlene's cousin survived the quake, but his wife did not. After the quake, Darlene moved back to her hometown to continue attending school.

Darlene returns to land to meet her family after spending ▶ nine days recovering on a medical ship.

Chapter 3

FORTUNATE TO BE ALIVE

*B*oom! Fourteen-year-old Sebastien Delatour was outside, studying for an upcoming school exam. He heard a sound like gunfire. What could it be? Next he heard his mother scream and run outside. He rushed inside. He ran up upstairs and found his sister, who had been taking a shower. She had fallen and hurt her head.

Sebastien's house did not fall down in the earthquake that day. The Delatours were better off than many Haitians. Their home was in a wealthy suburb of Port-au-Prince. It even had running water.

But Sebastien soon learned that his grandparents' house, in nearby Bourdon, was flattened by the quake. Sebastien's dad and uncles dug through the rubble for days. But they discovered both Carmelle and Cavour Delatour had been killed when the house fell.

◀ **Many survivors dug through rubble in search of loved ones after the earthquake.**

▲ **With many schools destroyed in Haiti, children attended classes in makeshift camps.**

Sebastien's family was devastated by the news. "My dad told me that he has to be strong for all of us," Sebastien recalled. "He can't show that he's crying. But I'm sure he did. . . . We all cried."[3]

In the days after the quake, the Delatour family reached out to victims of the disaster. Many of the family's relatives had lost their homes. Dozens came to stay with the Delatours. Sebastien searched for his classmates. One of his friend's fathers was killed. Another's home was destroyed. Many of Sebastien's peers were nowhere to be found.

Although Sebastien's school was still standing, the building was damaged. It was no longer safe to hold classes. The neighborhood around the Delatours' home was also dangerous because the nearby prison had been damaged. Criminals had escaped into the area. Sebastien's parents decided to send him to live with relatives in Miami, Florida. They wanted him to be away from danger and to go to school. When Sebastien heard this, he was not eager to leave. Sebastien knew he was fortunate to have family and a home. He saw the needs of the Haitian people. He wanted to stay for as long as he could. "I want to stay in Haiti and help give food and water to people," he said.[4]

EDUCATION BEFORE THE EARTHQUAKE

Haitians who did not finish sixth grade	**60%**
Teachers without adequate training	**75%**
Schools with electricity	**20%**
School-aged children enrolled in public schools	**20%**
Haitians unable to read or write	**38%**

Chapter 4

JUST GET ME OUT OF HERE!

Jillian Thorp was busy working in her office in Port-au-Prince when the building began to sway. It felt like she was having a dizzy spell. Then things started to fall off tables. Thorp's coworker pulled her under a doorframe. Ten seconds later, the building came down around them.

Twenty-three-year-old Thorp and her husband, Frank, were Americans living in Haiti as aid workers. Frank was in the mountains about 100 miles (161 km) away from the capital when the earthquake struck. It felt small from where he was. But he heard a rumor that Port-au-Prince was hit very hard. Frank was worried about his wife. He had to find out whether she was safe. He called her. "We're coming," he said.[5] Then, his phone died.

Meanwhile, Thorp was trapped in rubble from the waist down on the first floor of her building. A door had fallen above her and

◄ Strong earthquakes can easily reduce buildings to rubble.

her coworker, creating a sort of tent. This stopped the rubble from falling on them. Thorp's cell phone did not work when she tried to make a call. But she was able to receive calls. When friends from the United States called, she told them she was trapped. Then, she got the call from Frank. After about three hours, Thorp and her coworker heard people searching for them. Thorp cried out to let the rescuers know where she was.

The rescuers began to dig. Soon, they realized they could not save Thorp with their bare hands. There was too much broken concrete, metal, and wood for them to get through. They left to get better tools and more help.

After Frank's phone call to his wife was cut off, he drove for six hours through the night to get to her. He was shocked when he saw what the earthquake did to Port-au-Prince.

By the time Frank arrived, his wife had been trapped for nine hours. He jumped into the hole the rescuers had made. He could see only her hand waving up from below.

"Just get me out of here!" Thorp cried when she heard Frank was there.[6]

Frank and the others worked for more than an hour, pulling bricks, wood, and metal away from the site. Finally, they were

Rescuing survivors by hand was often a long, ▶ difficult process.

able to get Thorp and her coworker out. It had been ten hours since the quake.

Thorp was taken to a hospital in the Dominican Republic. The next day, she flew home to the United States. Being trapped in

AREAS HIT BY EARTHQUAKE

Cities across Haiti felt the earthquake at different intensities. The worst shaking occurred near the epicenter of the quake.

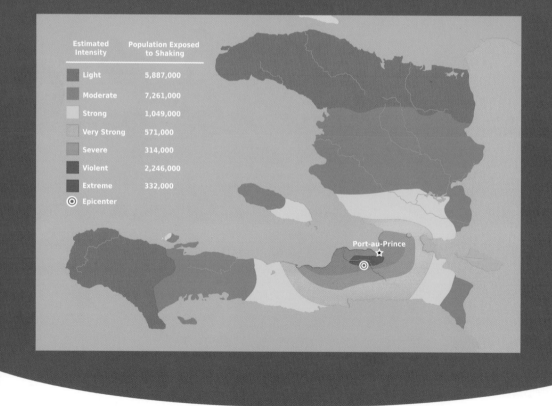

Estimated Intensity	Population Exposed to Shaking
Light	5,887,000
Moderate	7,261,000
Strong	1,049,000
Very Strong	571,000
Severe	314,000
Violent	2,246,000
Extreme	332,000
Epicenter	

Port-au-Prince

▲ Medical workers from around the world poured into Haiti to help care for those injured in the earthquake.

the debris had injured her legs. She had trouble walking for a while. She also had major bruises. But Thorp was grateful that her problems were small compared with the problems of many earthquake victims. After five weeks, she returned to Haiti to help. "I've just got to try. I've got to see if there's something still in me that I could [use to] help these people."[7]

Chapter 5

MIRACLE BOY

It was a normal afternoon in Port-au-Prince for seven-year-old Moise "Kiki" Joachin. He and his ten-year-old sister, Sabrina, were doing homework in their ground-floor apartment. His mother was making rice and beans for dinner. His father was at work at the Haiti customs office. His five-year-old brother had gone outside to get water, and his other three siblings played nearby.

Suddenly the building rattled and shook. Bricks and plaster fell all around. The entire six-story apartment building collapsed. Kiki was trapped beneath tons of broken concrete. He was not badly hurt, and he was able to breathe. But he could not get out. He was crammed with Sabrina and his brother Titite in a small open space under the rubble. They did not have any food or water. After five long days, Titite passed away.

On the eighth day, Kiki heard movement above the rubble. He cried out, asking for his mother and for water. Soon he heard

◀ **Many homes in Port-au-Prince did not have running water before the earthquake.**

voices and drills grinding through the concrete. After four hours, a hole opened up in the rubble. Kiki saw men wearing masks and hardhats. He was afraid at first. Then he heard his aunt's voice. She told him that the men were there to save him.

DEADLIEST EARTHQUAKES SINCE 1900

The location of the earthquake and conditions in the region made the 2010 Haiti earthquake the deadliest earthquake from 1900 to 2014.

Location	Date	Magnitude	Number of Deaths
Haiti	January 12, 2010	7.0	316,000
China	July 27, 1976	7.5	242,769
Indian Ocean	December 26, 2004	9.1	227,898
China	December 16, 1920	7.8	200,000
Japan	September 1, 1923	7.9	142,800

▲ **Kiki reacts as rescuers pull him and his sister from the rubble.**

Kiki let the rescue workers pull him out. His aunt was waiting for him and his sister. He was so happy to be out of the darkness. He smiled for the first time in eight days and raised his arms wide. Reporters at the scene photographed Kiki's big smile and outstretched arms. They wanted to show people that even in the sadness and devastation of the earthquake, there was good news. "I smiled because I was free," Kiki told the reporters. "I smiled because I was alive."[8] Newspapers published Kiki's story and called him the "miracle boy."

GLOSSARY

aftershocks (AF-ter-shahks): Aftershocks are smaller earthquakes that occur after a large quake. Many aftershocks occurred in the days following the 2010 Haiti earthquake.

debris (duh-BREE): Debris contains pieces of wreckage or broken things. Thousands of Haitians were trapped beneath debris after the earthquake.

dehydrated (dee-HYE-dray-tid): Someone who is dehydrated suffers from a lack of water. Darlene Etienne was dehydrated after two weeks without water.

devastation (dev-uh-STAY-shun): Devastation is extensive damage or destruction. Reporters in Haiti sent photographs to show the devastation caused by the earthquake.

epicenter (EP-i-sen-tur): The place on the earth's surface above the starting point of an earthquake is the epicenter. The epicenter of the Haiti earthquake was 10 miles (16 km) to the southwest of Port-au-Prince.

fault (fawlt): A fault is a crack in the earth's crust. Experts know a major fault runs through Port-au-Prince.

interpreter (in-TUR-prit-ur): An interpreter is a person who translates for those who speak different languages. Junior Bernard worked as an interpreter for U.S. workers in Haiti.

poverty (PAH-vur-tee): Poverty is the state of having little or no money. Most of the Haitians in Port-au-Prince lived in poverty.

rubble (RUHB-uhl): Rubble is the concrete, bricks, and stones from a broken building. Many people were trapped under rubble after the earthquake in Haiti.

SOURCE NOTES

1. Kimberly Davidow. "Haitian Man's Survival Story Launches His Journey to Reading." *WFMZ News*. Marathon Broadcasting Company, Inc., 7 Feb. 2013. Web. 24 Jun. 2015.

2. "Bathwater Saves Haiti Survivor after 15 Days." *Metro*. Associated Newspapers Limited., 29 Feb. 2010. Web. 24 Jun. 2015.

3. Valerie Moore. "Sebastien's Story: A Young Haitian Earthquake Survivor Speaks." *UNICEF*. United Nations., 21 Jan. 2010. Web. 24 Jun. 2015.

4. Ibid.

5. Cathy Herholdt. "Staff Profile: Jillian Thorp's Story of Survival." *Humanitarian Aid & Relief*. World Concern., 23 Jul. 2010. Web. 24 Jun. 2015.

6. "Hero Husband Helps Dig Out Wife in Haiti." *CBS News*. CBS Interactive Inc., 13 Jan. 2010. Web. 24 Jun. 2015.

7. Cathy Herholdt. "Staff Profile: Jillian Thorp's Story of Survival." *Humanitarian Aid & Relief*. World Concern., 23 Jul. 2010. Web. 24 Jun. 2015.

8. Matthew McDermott. "Kiki's Rescue." *Pictures of the Year International.* Donald W. Reynolds Journalism Institute., n.d. Web. 24 Jun. 2015.

TO LEARN MORE

Books

Benoit, Peter. *The Haitian Earthquake of 2010*. New York: Scholastic, 2011.

Murray, Peter. *Earthquakes*. Mankato, MN: Child's World, 2015.

Ventura, Marne. *How to Survive an Earthquake*. Mankato, MN: Child's World, 2016.

Web Sites

Visit our Web site for links about the Haiti earthquake:
childsworld.com/links

Note to Parents, Teachers, and Librarians: We routinely verify our Web links to make sure they are safe and active sites. So encourage your readers to check them out!

INDEX